SKARA BRAE

NORTHERN EUROPE'S BEST PRESERVED NEOLITHIC VILLAGE

DAVID CLARKE
Keeper of Archaeology,
National Museums of Scotland
and
PATRICK MAGUIRE

In the winter of 1850 a wild storm stripped the grass from the high dune known as Skara Brae in the Bay of Skaill on mainland Orkney. An immense midden or refuse heap was uncovered. So too were the ruins of ancient dwellings. What came to light in that storm proved to be the best preserved neolithic village in northern Europe. And it remains that today.

The village of Skara Brae was inhabited before the Egyptian pyramids were built, and flourished many centuries before construction began at Stonehenge. It is some 5000 years old.

But it is not its age alone that makes it so remarkable and so important. It is the degree to which it has been preserved.

The structures of this semi-subterranean village survive in impressive condition. And so, amazingly, does the furniture in the village houses. Nowhere else in northern Europe are we able to see such rich evidence of how our remote ancestors actually lived.

The profound importance of this remarkable site was given official recognition in 1999 when it was inscribed upon the World Heritage List as part of the Heart of Neolithic Orkney World Heritage Site.

Published by HISTORIC SCOTLAND
Edited by Chris Tabraham, designed by The Marketing & Design Agency.
Principal photography by Michael Brooks and Ian Larner.
Photographs of the objects are reproduced by kind permission of the Trustees of the National Museums of Scotland.
Drawings by Bil Fulton, Ross Gillespie and Jim Proudfoot.
Crown Copyright © Historic Scotland 2000.
Reprinted 2004 & 2007 in Scotland from sustainable materials by The House, Edinburgh

ISBN 1 900168 97 9

A GUIDED TOUR

This tour takes you round the village, pointing out features of special interest. It i designed to help you make some sense of what you are seeing.

There are eight viewing points, indicated by markers set into the ground. As you mov round, different aspects of the village are briefly commented upon.

The guidebook then deals with some of the curiosities and questions that visiting th remarkable village may have provoked.

Aerial view of Skara Brae
(copyright Gunnie Moberg)

A plan of the village

Suggested route
Information panel
House numbers

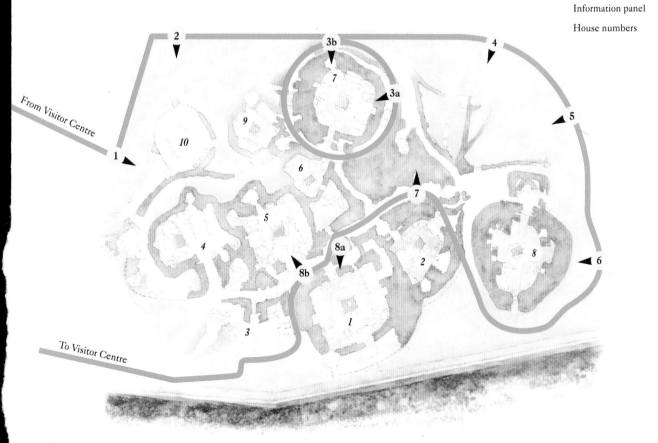

From Visitor Centre

To Visitor Centre

VIEWING POINT 1

Skara Brae had two phases. Most of what we see belongs to the second and later phase of the village. Below that there are the remains of an earlier village laid out on a different plan.

The doorway and stump of wall we are looking at here, on the edge of the settlement as it's now exposed, is part of the earlier village because it's built on a lower level. However, just not enough is visible to say what it formed part of.

To see more we would have to excavate further. But to do that we would have to demolish a large part of House 4.

VIEWING POINT 2

In certain places we can see earlier houses, preserved because they didn't have a later house built on top of them. Below us is House 9, the better preserved of the earlier houses still to be seen.

We can see the central hearth, remains of a dresser, and beds on either side. The beds are set into the thickness of the walls rather than projecting out from them. This is the only difference in design from the later houses.

Turning slightly right, we see House 10, a much less well-preserved earlier house. It has been very badly robbed – maybe to provide building stone for the later village. Indeed, it wouldn't be easily recognised for what it is if we didn't have House 9.

VIEWING POINT 3

Here we are looking into House 7, best preserved of all the houses. Its dresser, box beds, hearth and storage spaces are all standard features of Skara Brae houses.

We are standing above the dresser looking towards the narrow doorway.

The penned-off area by the doorway was probably used for storing large pots – to prevent them being kicked or otherwise accidentally damaged.

The reconstructed house at the Visitor Centre is based on House 7.

VIEWING POINT 4

We see the wall running round from the entrance to the main passage separating the mound of midden that cocooned the semi-subterranean houses of the village from the workshop (see Viewing Point 6). The walls in the foreground divide areas used for other activities. What activities? We don't know.

VIEWING POINT 5

Here we are looking down into the main passage. The passages allowed access to the semi-subterranean houses of the village through the mound of midden* that cocooned them from the elements.

This midden isn't the built-up everyday refuse of the village but was dumped there earlier as the first stage of building the village itself. The passages, though now open, would have been roofed over – as we can still see, looking further along.

* Midden: a mixture of decomposed vegetable matter, animal dung, broken animal bones, stone and shells. The material is more or less the same as that produced by a gardener's compost heap. It has the texture of very tough clay.

VIEWING POINT 6

Before us is Structure 8. This is the only
building in the settlement that isn't a house.
No beds, no dresser. There is, however, a central hearth.

The walls are much thicker here because this building was not
surrounded by midden. It was always free-standing. So the walls had to be much
sturdier to support the roof.

Information gathered during its excavation suggests this was a workshop – chiefly
for making stone tools.

VIEWING POINT 7

Here we see the entrance to the main
passage. The stone-faced walls on either side
marked the edge of the midden mound, and
created a clear boundary between the living-
quarters and areas outside.

VIEWING POINT 8

As we face the sea, in front of us is House 1. This shows the basic layout of all houses in the village. The door is beneath us.

Opposite us is the dresser – where prized objects were stored and displayed. Around the dresser, set into the floor, are three small tanks for preparing fish bait. Just to the right of the dresser is a large grinding stone.

In the centre is the hearth. Between the hearth and the dresser is a stone seat.

On either side of the house are box beds. Above the beds, set into the walls are further storage spaces. Yet more storage is provided by cells or alcoves set into the thickness of the walls.

Now, if we turn right round and look into House 5 we see two of these cells more clearly: one set into the wall behind the less well-preserved dresser, and another whose entrance is in the corner of the house.

The cell behind the dresser is typical of many in the houses. Blocked by what was stored in the dresser, access to this cell would have been difficult – and so things could have been stored here quite securely. Other cells, less hidden, would have had more regular uses.

ABOUT THIS BOOKLET

Now you've seen Skara Brae, we can try to deal with some of the curiosities and questions that experiencing this remarkable village may have provoked.

We approach these questions on two levels.

On the first level we offer you what experts think is unquestionably true of the village and the life of its people.

On the second level we offer the best guesses we can make about aspects of village life – saying what we think most probable in the light of other discoveries about early farming communities on Orkney and elsewhere in Britain. On this level there can be no certainty – only likelihood.

We distinguish between these two levels typographically: undoubted fact is printed in normal type; speculation is presented in *italic type*.

Skara Brae at the edge of the Bay of Skaill with the hills of Hoy in the background

SKARA BRAE:
ONE OF THE EARLIEST FARMING VILLAGES

Skara Brae is one of the first known farming villages in Britain. Most other early settlements of farmers are single farmsteads, *perhaps situated quite closely together* but not, as here, forming a well-integrated, closely-knit community properly deserving the name 'village'. So Skara Brae marks a real departure from previous ways of living.

THE PRESERVATION OF SKARA BRAE

Skara Brae has been well preserved for two reasons.

First, the structures of the village are built into, and are surrounded by, midden. This has acted as a strong protecting agent. Midden is formed, for the most part, from the decomposition of organic matter, much as in a gardener's compost heap. It also contains ash, shells, broken bones, stone and other waste from everyday activities. Textured like tough clay, it makes impressively durable building material.

Second, the sand that filled up and buried the village after its abandonment gave everything a formidable stability – just as sandbagging absorbs explosive blast.

But, despite this excellent protection by midden and sand, we still can't be sure whether we're looking at a small village, virtually intact – or at what survives of a larger village.

Great storms, like the one that first partially exposed the site in 1850, may have eroded the seaward side of the village long before people would have been interested to examine what those storms were uncovering.

On the other hand, archaeologists are fairly confident that, landward, little, if anything, remains to be discovered.

Happily, by 1850, there had grown up sufficient archaeological awareness and scientific curiosity to encourage the laird of Skaill, William Watt, to explore what that year's storm had revealed.

After the great storm of 1850

ABOUT THE HOUSES

The floor area of the houses is some 36 square metres compared with the 61.5 square metres of a modern two-bedroomed semi-detached house or apartment in Britain today. So, the houses are quite spacious – although, being just one room, they may not appear so. It is perhaps worth noting that the small size of the house doorways doesn't mean that the people themselves were small – merely that small doorways offer good draught-proofing from Orcadian winds.

THE ROOFS

Because of the state of preservation of the houses and the way they are displayed today – we must look down into them – it may be easy to forget that, originally, these houses were roofed. *The beams supporting the timber roof would have been whalebone or timber – perhaps varying from house to house, depending on what was available.*

The roofs themselves were probably made from turf, held down by a network of weighted ropes of twisted heather. Had they been made from flagstone the excavators would have expected to find fragments of stone where roofs had collapsed. They found none. This, however, doesn't rule out stone roofing – it just makes it unlikely.

Inside House 7

THE FURNITURE

The furniture in the village houses was made largely from stone. And this for two related reasons.

First, Orkney, then as now, was almost without trees – certainly trees large enough to provide timber in bulk.

Second, the nature of the local flagstone, its ready availability, its easy workability, makes it ideal construction material for most purposes.

Not that the people of Skara Brae didn't have wood to work with. Considerable quantities of driftwood from the eroding virgin forests of North America would have been washed up on the island beaches, carried across the Atlantic by the prevailing currents. But wood would have been needed to make those items for which stone isn't suitable: boats, roofing timbers, and such fundamental things as tool handles.

Box bed

THE BEDS

Today we see only the skeletons of the people's box beds, the stone remains. *Bracken would have served as a form of mattress; sheepskins and other animal skins would have been used as blankets. Pillars would have risen from the front ends of the beds, supporting a canopy of skin or wood tied back to the walls of the house. Like some very early four-poster, curtains of skins may have draped down from the canopy, enclosing the beds for greater warmth.*

Perhaps the canopy was designed to protect the sleeper from a roof not quite weatherproof. And, if the canopy were made from plants, or had some wooden supporting component, space on top could have been used for storage.

Usually, the beds have cupboards set into the wall above them *for keeping personal effects.*

THE DRESSER

In each house, the dresser faces the door, and dominates your view as you enter. This may have been a simple storage unit. *But it could have provided a place of display, something like today's mantlepiece or sideboard, where a family's – or an individual's – prized belongings could be arrayed.*

There is a stone seat in front of the dresser in the best preserved houses.

Dresser

CENTRAL HEARTH

In the centre of the house between the door and the dresser is the hearth. But what did the people burn in it? While there is plenty of usable peat in Orkney today, this didn't form until several centuries after the settlement was abandoned. *Fuel was probably a mixture of animal dung, dried seaweed, heather, bracken, and marine mammal bone (rich in oil) – such as whalebone.*

They also may have burned some wood. But not much. Virtually no charcoal has been found. Wood was probably too precious to burn.

Central hearth

THE BOXES

Set into the floors of the houses, near the hearth, are stone boxes. The joints of these boxes were luted – cemented with clay – to make them watertight.

In these boxes limpets were soaked to be used as fish bait. Limpets are effective fish bait but they need to be softened before fish find them tempting. Soaking achieves this. But it takes time. So, to have a constant supply of fresh bait on hand, several smaller boxes are used in rotation, rather than using one large tank where it is difficult to know which limpets have already been softened.

Storage boxes

THE CELLS

These are cupboards, alcoves, or compartments recessed into the walls of the houses. They vary in size, and in ease of access. Some cells are handy; others – such as those behind the dressers – are quite hard to get at.

Most of these are storage spaces. *It seems probable that items of most value were stored in the least accessible cells.*

The merits of using midden to build the walls is shown again here. Some of the cells are fairly large; to set these into walls of dry stone would mean building extremely thick walls.

Some cells – never more than one in any house – have drains running underneath them. *These seem to be indoor toilets.* But, because the drains can't be fully mapped without demolishing structures built above them, it can't be said definitely that every house had one. From what evidence we have, however, this seems more likely than not. Indeed, insofar as the excavation of the drains has been possible, we could be seeing one of the earliest comprehensive systems of indoor sanitation.

Inside a cell

THE DOORS

The doors were not hinged. We can still see the two doorstops: one projecting from the floor, the other from the ceiling of the entrance passage. The door itself was a slab of stone or wood, large enough to fill the entrance gap. The door was pinned against the projecting stops by a bar crossing behind it and fitting into slots in the wall of the entrance passage. This allowed the door to be opened and closed. The bars were made of whalebone or wood.

An existing doorway

How it might have looked with door in place

CARVINGS

Carvings decorate some of the stones in the walls of some houses and passages. The patterns are geometric, abstract in design. *These probably had meaning for the villagers, but we have no idea what this may have been. The carvings may have been coloured – there is no reason to suppose they were just bare marks.*

Decorated stone

IN THE MIDDEN

Midden was extremely important in building the later semi-subterranean village of Skara Brae; the houses were deliberately encased in it; the passages were cut through it. Since using midden as a building material is unfamiliar to us, it's perhaps worth saying a little about how it was produced and used.

The people living in the earlier village purposefully collected their everyday refuse on a nearby site where, after gradual decomposition, midden formed.

When sufficient midden had accumulated the villagers gathered together mounds of it and deposited these wherever they wished to build. Next, they dug holes in the mounds to situate new houses and passages. Finally, they put into place the stones for the structures. At no point was the later village ever a collection of free-standing structures.

Now, why did they build in this way? Midden wasn't essential for making buildings stand up. They could build free-standing stone buildings when they chose to. The Workshop (Structure 8) stands up and it isn't surrounded by midden.

Using midden may have to do with wind-proofing and general weatherproofing. The sinuous passage (easier to build with the support of midden) seems designed to throw the wind away from the doors of the dwellings. Moreover, the semi-subterranean design with its single entrance makes it easier to keep straying animals – like dogs – out of the village.

The midden, fronted by the dry stone walls, clearly marks off the human dwellings from the rest of the village. This, together with the stereotyped design of the houses themselves – they are all more or less built to the same plan – may give us some clue to the nature of community attitudes.

A SENSE OF COMMUNITY

Nowadays we lay out our living spaces more or less as we choose. In Skara Brae they didn't: *this was a community where there was a single way of arranging the interior of the house. This suggests a conforming community – people doing things in the same way because sharing attitudes and beliefs is seen as very important for living together in harmony.*

The midden may have had symbolic meaning for the people. It may have seemed to them a physical sign of the strong sense of identity within their community, binding them together, fixing their boundaries: in here we live – out there is the rest of the world.

Yet there are no communal dwellings. This is different. *Within this community exists a notion of privacy. The houses are private houses, for family units. Two generations, parents and their children – some grandparents possibly – but not aunts, uncles, cousins and so on.*

The houses clustered together, surrounded by midden

THE WORKSHOP

This free-standing structure was built on a different plan from the houses. The walls are much thicker. They had to be – to give stability to the structure, as there was no supporting midden. Inside, although there is a central hearth, the structure has none of the other features we find in the houses: no dresser, no beds, no boxes, no cells.

When it was excavated the floor was littered with fragments of chert – a flint-like stone. *This suggests it was a workshop, a place for craft activities, and the chert fragments are debris from making stone tools.*

The workshop

THE 'MARKETPLACE'

The paved area outside the workshop, which has been called the 'marketplace', was paved *simply because it was situated by the entrance to the main passage into the village. Exposed to the elements, it would take a lot of wear and tear from people coming and going, especially in bad weather.* There is nothing to suggest this was, in fact, a marketplace.

THE PASSAGES

Two passages remain: the main passage, and one branching off at right angles in the direction of House 7. How many there were originally isn't known. *If the village had been larger than we see it today there probably would have been other branch passages since the passages were constructed simply to link the houses within the village.* The passages were roofed with stone slabs and then covered in midden.

Again, it is worth saying that the height of the passages improved windproofing.

Inside the main passage

THE WAY OF LIFE AT SKARA BRAE

HEATING

The central hearth would have heated the houses – as well as providing the cooking facility. The design of the village would have minimised heat loss so the houses could have been kept comfortable quite efficiently.

LIGHTING

The houses would have been very dark had there been no interior lighting except that radiating from the fire in the hearth. And no surviving objects resemble lamps. But we can't say with certainty there were no lamps. *If there were lamps of some sort these could have burned oil taken from marine mammals or seabirds.* Whatever the case, the light in the houses wouldn't have been strong – never matching the level produced by gas lamps for example.

VENTILATION

There would have been little ventilation. The air inside the houses would have been very smoky. (This could have allowed food to have been smoked in the roof.) There may have been a hole in the roof to let smoke out. But, if not, it is unlikely the roofs were fitted so tightly as to prevent any ventilation.

REFUSE DISPOSAL

The villagers would have cleared out their houses from time to time in the normal way, building up a midden heap somewhere outside the village – we don't know where. *This may be part of the settlement lost through storm damage.* At Noltland, a site similar to Skara Brae on the Orcadian island of Westray, a huge area of midden (some 1100 square metres) has been uncovered.

THE VILLAGE BENEATH THE VILLAGE AT SKARA BRAE

The village of Skara Brae was continuously inhabited for some 600 years (about 3100 BC-2500 BC). And this period of habitation falls into two overlapping but distinct phases. What we see today is – apart from two earlier houses – the remains of the village from the second phase of its occupation.

This drawing shows – in section – how the later village stands on the remains of the earlier

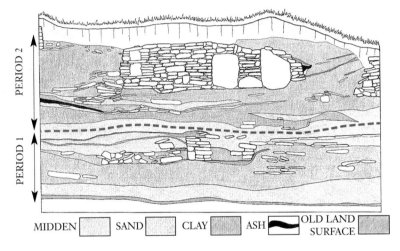

About half-way through the occupation of the site, the descendants of the first settlers decided to improve their dwellings. Over time, this amounted to building a new village on the same site. It is clear from relics discovered during excavation that the builders of the second village were the same people as those who had lived in the first village. *The period of rebuilding may have taken up to a generation to complete.*

The later village was built on the gradually levelled remains of the earlier village. But it wasn't laid out according to the same plan. So we can't say that there was an earlier house immediately below any house we see today. Indeed, this is why we can still see the two earlier houses – because no later structures were built on top of them. These two houses were found

buried in the midden mound, covering the entire dwelling area, into which the second, later village was built. The full extent of the mound has never been completely excavated.

The later houses were built more or less to the same specifications as the earlier houses – but the second-phase houses are larger. And there is one noticeable design difference; in the earlier period the beds were recessed into the walls of the houses rather than projecting into the living space. Otherwise, the two designs are the same.

The earlier buildings were sunk into a certain amount of midden but they were much more free-standing than those of the later village. *Perhaps what enabled the building of the later village was the accumulation of sufficient midden for the improved design to be feasible – since building in midden lends support to structures and so allows larger buildings to be constructed more easily.*

THE GEOGRAPHY OF SKARA BRAE

Over the past 5000 years the geography of the Skara Brae area has changed in only one important respect. Now just a small stretch of sand stands between the village and the sea – and, in winter, sometimes barely that, for the Bay of Skaill is often visited by tremendous storms throwing large boulders and great heaps of seaweed over the seawall into the site. But when the village was occupied, it was some distance from the sea.

In even earlier times, a freshwater loch lay where the Bay is, separated from the sea by a ridge of cliffs running across what is now the Bay's mouth. Looking seawards, it is easy to make out what remains of that protective wall jutting out into the bay like the horns of a crescent moon.

Gradually the cliffs were eroded by storms, and the freshwater loch drained out into the sea. Sand dunes formed. And these are what separated the village from the sea when it was inhabited. Later, from these dunes came the sand that filled up and buried the village after it had been abandoned.

Not much else has changed. The surrounds of the village were then much as now: established pasture land. Remove the modern structures – the houses, the present field walls – and little would be different. In some nearby fields cereal would have been cultivated. Where exactly those fields were we don't know – but traces of cereals have been found in the village.

At that time the area's average temperature was probably a degree or two higher than it is now and so the climate could have supported the growing of such cereals as wheat and barley. Today, even with modern farming methods and improved crop strains, to do this economically is too difficult to be practical.

An impression of how the village might have looked when inhabited
(Jim Proudfoot)

THEIR WORK

The people of Skara Brae were farmers and fishermen.

THEIR FARMING

They kept cattle and a few pigs. They also kept sheep or goats – it is impossible from bone remains to say which. They may have kept both.

They grew crops, chiefly barley, but also some wheat. They didn't have ploughs like those used today. Theirs was a type of light plough called an ard – a sharply-pointed tool suitable for cutting grooves in the light sandy soil of the area, grooves into which the seed was thrown before it was covered over again using a harrow. It isn't possible to say whether ards were drawn by animals or people.

THEIR FISHING

We don't know a great deal about their fishing. Almost no fishing tackle has been found in the material recovered from the site. But a large amount of fishbone has been identified – mainly cod and saithe. *This suggests most of their fishing was coastal.*

Some whalebone – though not a lot – has been found, most of it fashioned into various tools. They also burned it. Very little waste whalebone remained. *Since the sea was some distance from the village, whales would have been stripped near the sea's edge and only useful bone carried back to the village.*

So, did they hunt whales? No tools for killing whales have been found. *This suggests the bone came from beached whales.* On the other hand, pilot whales can be driven into shallow water and then clubbed to death – a practice still seen in the Faroe Islands today.

Pig

Whale

THEIR LEISURE

Every natural society engages in leisure activities – but Skara Brae offers little evidence of what its people's pursuits may have been. There are a pair of bone objects which look like they may have been used as a type of dice. Also, found together were a number of cow knucklebones which, just conceivably, may have been used in some tossing or throwing game, or in some form of ritual – possibly divination.

THEIR TOOL KIT

There was no knowledge of metal in the New Stone Age. People made their tools from stone – mainly from flint, or, occasionally, from chert. The structure of flint resembles that of glass. It's easily flaked and easily shaped. And it's good for making tools with very sharp cutting edges.

At Skara Brae stone tools were found. These were made mostly from local chert. There were also some flint tools. This flint had been formed in chalk beds under the North Sea and nodules of it, gradually eroded by the action of currents, were thrown up as pebbles on local beaches.

But the people faced considerable problems. The flint pebbles were small: so the tools that could be made from them had to be small also. Furthermore, the people had no control over the regularity or quantity of the sea-borne supply of flint.

Orcadian chert is inferior to flint. It doesn't make such a good tool – it can't be given as sharp a cutting edge. People would only use chert when flint wasn't available. And, again, there is a problem of size with the chert in Orkney. It doesn't occur in large blocks and so couldn't be made into the large tools the people needed.

To overcome the problems of supply and size of stone, the people adopted a two-stage process of tool-making.

Microscopic analysis of stone tools can show what materials those tools were used to work. And such analysis tells us that here the stone tools were used to work bone and wood – although we see little wood since it doesn't preserve well.

In effect, what the people did was first use their limited supply of stone to make stone tools, and then, in turn, use these stone tools to fashion locally available bone and wood into a second, more comprehensive set of tools – including the larger tools they needed.

The bone came from the larger animals in their herds, and from marine mammals. A whalebone rib, for example, is large, strong, and dense enough to provide suitable material for making efficient, sizeable tools.

So, while the fundamental tool kit of

New Stone Age people elsewhere was made largely from stone, at Skara Brae it was made from bone – and wood. A great variety of tools not seen outside Orkney has been recovered from the site.

So what were these tools used for? We have to bear in mind that tools may not be made for one purpose only. Or if a tool is made for a specific task that doesn't mean it won't be used for other tasks as well. We need only think of the number of uses today's screwdriver is put to.

At Skara Brae the range of tools is wide. But bone tools, unlike stone, can't be analysed to discover what materials they were used to work. So we have to guess. And remember each tool could have been put to more than one use.

For example, there are bone points obviously suitable for leatherworking – for punching holes and stitching; but these points may have also been used to tease out crabmeat. Then again, there are bone slices, probably used for scraping skins, but also capable of use as cutting tools. And there are bone mattocks, probably used for cutting the ground, but perhaps also used to strip blubber from whales.

Bone awl made from the leg-bone of an adult gannet

Two stone axe-heads, a bone point and the bone head of a mattock

WHAT THEY ATE

We face a problem trying to say what the villagers ate. Vegetable matter does not preserve as well as animal. So, while there is plenty of evidence to tell us about its meat content, little remains to help us detail what part fruits and cereals played in the diet.

However, we do know they cultivated barley and a little wheat. *They may have baked bread.* Small ovens have been found at Rinyo, on the Orcadian island of Rousay, a settlement similar in date and character to Skara Brae. *In all likelihood they collected wild plants, herbs, fruits and nuts. They may have brewed alcoholic 'beers' by fermenting local plants.*

On the other hand, it is clear that their diet was richly endowed with meats of land and sea. Many meat and seafood eaters today might well envy them this menu: MEAT – Beef, lamb, pork, venison, goat. FISH AND SEAFOOD – Cod, saithe, lobster, crab, mussels, sea urchin, oysters, whale and seal meat.

Perhaps their taste for the flesh and eggs of seabirds – eider duck, great auk, gannet, guillemot, shag – seems a little less desirable.

Salt would have come from evaporating seawater.

From nearby streams they would have had fresh water to drink. They would also have had cows' milk, ewes' milk and goats' milk – as well as their 'beers'. *And perhaps they made cheese and other milk products.*

Hazel Nuts

Razorbills

Large Cod

Red Deer

WHAT THEY WORE

No clothing survives. All we can say is that, since no tools related to spinning or weaving have been found, they were probably not producing textiles – *although techniques of felt-making may have been known. So we must guess that their clothes were made from the skins and furs of the animals they kept or hunted, including the fur of otter and other small mammals not likely to have been sought for their meat (pine marten bones have been discovered at a site on the island of Westray). They may also have* used down to add warmth to their clothing.

These clothes may well have been tailored to some degree of sophistication, for amongst the tools found there are many that seem specially suited for working skins.

Their clothes may have been decorated with beads. So many beads were found at Skara Brae, many of them were used to make items of jewellery. *Some beads may well have been sewn on garments in a type of appliqué decoration.*

THEIR JEWELLERY

Three types of jewellery have been found: beads, pendants and pins – almost all made from bone. But also surviving are part of one wooden pin, and a few stone beads.

The beads, ranging in size, *would have been strung together to form necklaces, bracelets, armlets and the like. Most of the pendants, made from the teeth of marine mammals, may have been part of these personal ornaments, strung alongside the beads. But some pendants are so finely decorated that these were probably strung separately.*

The pins vary in length from that of one of today's hairpins to some 350mm. Many of these pins are carved from walrus tusk *(walrus may have been breeding on Orkney at the time).* Some pins have been deliberately given a blackish hue. This shade was achieved by heating the bone under controlled conditions and is evidence that the villagers didn't restrict themselves to naturally-occurring colours.

Indeed, colour may have been widely used in ornament. For also found on the site were 'paint pots', made variously from oyster shells, whale vertebrae and stone. In these, red ochre was ground up; and in one of the pots, a ball of paste was found, composed of ochre and fat. Whether this mixing of colour was for body decoration or for colouring carvings, or both, it is impossible to say.

Pots made of stone, bone and shell containing ochre

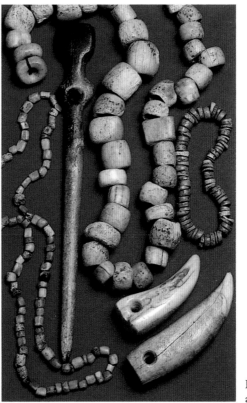

Bone beads, pins and pendants

MEDICINE, RELIGION AND LAW

THEIR MEDICINE

We have only one piece of evidence that suggests a specific herbal medicine – *although it is likely the people collected many herbs and plants for medicinal purposes.*

The outer skins of a kind of puffball – Bovista nigrescens – were found in such numbers that it is clear the inhabitants had purpose for these fungi. The inner tissue of the puffball resembles cotton wool. When applied to minor cuts, it acts as a blood-clotting agent.

Puffballs similar to those collected by the inhabitants of Skara Brae

THEIR RELIGIOUS BELEIFS

It is impossible to know what the people believed in. *But we can guess they practised some form of ancestor worship.* On Orkney, as in many other parts of Britain during the New Stone Age, a considerable amount of energy was spent constructing chamber tombs (an estimated average of 10,000 working hours on each tomb). This leads us to believe that the ancestors held a special position in the lives of the people.

The ancestors would have been consulted – through some form of ritual contact – for advice on everyday problems of village life. They would have been asked to speak to the gods on the villagers' behalf in times of family difficulty or community crisis.

LAW

No formal laws as we understand them governed the villagers. Custom and tradition would have guided community life. *Any conflict that couldn't be settled by argument or debate would have been resolved by appealing for a decision to village ancestors.*

Special stone objects, probably used in religious rites

CONTACT WITH OTHER SETTLEMENTS

From what we know of Skara Brae we can say that the village was self-sufficient, able to meet its basic needs. But there is evidence to suggest that its people engaged in exchanges with other villages.

For example, pieces of haematite, a valuable iron ore, have been found on the site. *Haematite was probably used as a tool for finishing leather, putting a high polish on the skin. It only occurs in two veins on the north coast of the island of Hoy.*

It now seems likely that the people of Skara Brae didn't travel for this material but obtained

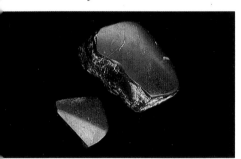
Haematite

it in exchange for some item of value to which they had local access.

A further reason for contact with other villages would be to arrange marriage partners. The villages weren't large enough to permit exclusively internal marriages without running risk of genetic damage through inbreeding. (A rough estimate of the size of Skara Brae would say there were probably never more than about 20 families living in the settlement – even allowing that large amounts of the village might have been washed away in storms.)

Contact between communities may also have occurred when small-to-medium size religious monuments were being built, such as village chamber tombs like those at Wideford Hill and Cuween Hill on Mainland Orkney. Each village would have had a chamber tomb, where its ancestors were buried; and each could have supplied enough labour to build its own. But, remembering the amount of time needed for such constructions, it is more likely that, to help speed such tasks, villages would lend each other labour.

VILLAGE LEADERS

Skara Brae was a community of families, recognising family structure and some measure of family privacy. It was also a tightly-knit community held together by strongly-shared beliefs, activities and goals. The houses do not vary in layout, nor sufficiently in size, to allow us to believe that this was a community composed of a 'chieftain' and his followers.

The village seems to have been an 'egalitarian' society. Leadership was neither hereditary nor all embracing. There would have been leaders of a kind, though – individuals, who because of their skills in a particular activity, led the people while they were carrying out that activity.

There may have been a 'fishing leader', a 'farming leader', and so on. These would have been the people who knew most, and were best at, that particular communal activity. Indeed, the curious, highly-decorated stone objects found on

the site may have been associated with these various leaders. But there wouldn't have been an overall leader within the community.

OTHER COMMUNITIES ON ORKNEY AT THE TIME OF SKARA BRAE

Skara Brae remained a unique site on Orkney from its exposure in 1850 until a second settlement was discovered at Rinyo just before World War II. At that time it was still thought that such settlements would prove very rare. But, between 1976 and 2000, three further villages of similar character have been found, and now it appears more may come to light.

TOWARDS THE END ...

Towards the end of the occupation of Skara Brae the inhabitants of the Orcadian villages were coming together to build bigger and more elaborate monuments. The splendid chamber tomb at Maes Howe is an example of one type of this large-scale building.

Other types are the important religious henge monuments and stone circles like those at Stenness and Ring of Brogar.

(A henge may be loosely described as a circular area defined by a bank and ditch.)

It is estimated that, in all, almost 150,000 hours of work were needed to construct Stenness and Ring of Brogar, very much more than any single village could have supported. To build on such a scale would have required quite a degree of organised, co-ordinated effort.

Maes Howe

Ring of Brogar

Entrance passage at Maes Howe

... A NEW ORDER

This large-scale building is evidence for a new order governing the social relationships between the villages, and, ultimately, causing major changes within the villages themselves.

Instead of more or less self-contained 'egalitarian' villages we now see a regional group emerging, whose leaders exert growing religious and political power over the constituent communities.

As well as organising major building projects, these leaders would have taken on the task of communicating with the ancestors on the people's behalf – becoming in the process the 'court' through whose decisions conflicts would have been settled. The new order would have rendered the village chamber tombs unnecessary.

Maes Howe would have been built to replace the older village chamber tombs, and provide a burial place for the leaders of the regional group. The form of the tomb would still have been familiar, acceptable to the people. But the scale now is much grander.

SKARA BRAE ABANDONED

The emergence of the regional group may have been a major force causing the breakdown of the older community organisation which had flourished in self-governing villages such as Skara Brae.

The new order may have led people to question the need for living in tightly-knit villages. The balance between the needs of the single family unit and collective village purpose – as reflected in the physical layout of Skara Brae – may well have been upset by the establishment of the regional group.

The individual family would have become more important, village organisation less so; and people would have gone back to living in dispersed single farmsteads, each now seeing itself as part of, and identifying with, the regional group. So, gradually, Skara Brae, and the other villages, would have been abandoned.

It must be said that this is not the traditional explanation of why Skara Brae was abandoned. Professor Childe, the principal excavator of the site, believed that the people left the village after a huge sandstorm had inundated their houses. But

Childe's view is open to question on two accounts.

First, if the people had been forced out by a sandstorm why didn't they return and dig out the sand from the undamaged stone structures? Second, excavators didn't find sand to a depth any greater than one metre – a level more consistent with its being gradually blown into the village after it was abandoned than with sand causing the abandonment.

While it isn't possible to rule out completely some type of catastrophe suddenly forcing the people to leave the village, there is no satisfactory evidence to support any such view.

It seems more likely desertion took place over a longer period of time – the village slowly falling into disuse when the younger, more adventurous people moved out to single farmsteads as the idea of regional organisation took over. These people weren't replaced; and the more conservative element left behind would have eventually died out.

HOW THE STORY CAME TO LIGHT

Professor Gordon Childe at Skara Brae, 1930

Excavations on the edge of the village, 1972

Excavations in the village, 1972

In the winter of 1850 an extremely severe storm stripped the grass from the high dune known as Skara Brae in the south corner of the Bay of Skaill. The storm exposed an immense midden mound or refuse heap and the ruins of ancient dwellings.

The laird of Skaill, William Watt, began to explore the site and by 1868, four of the houses had been cleared out and a very rich collection of objects had been lodged in Skaill House.

The site was then left undisturbed, apart from some casual digging, until the end of 1925. Then in December of that year another terrific storm washed away part of the midden mound and damaged part of the previously cleared structures.

At that time the ruins had only just been placed under the guardianship of the Commissioners of HM Office of Works by William Watt's trustees. So, to prevent further storm damage, the Commissioners had the present sea-wall built, securing the foundations of the site. Later, the buildings were strengthened and consolidated.

Soon after this work was begun in 1927 it was discovered that there were further undisturbed structures buried beneath the midden. Professor Gordon Childe was called in to supervise the archaeological aspects of work on the site. And between 1928 and 1930, the rest of the dwellings that make up the site today were cleared out.

In 1972 and 1973 further excavation was carried out to gain further information about the site's environment and the life of the village people. Samples were collected – for radiocarbon dating and other analytic procedures not known in Childe's time or much improved since then.

Analysis of the large number of finds from this work is still continuing but, where possible, conclusions are incorporated in the information given here.

SOME COMMONLY ASKED QUESTIONS

In the course of this booklet we have tried to anticipate the questions that might have aroused your curiosity. Inevitably, there will be matters we've missed out. But here are some final best guesses in answer to some stray questions commonly asked by visitors to Skara Brae.

What did the people look like?

We have no reason to believe that the people of Skara Brae looked any different from people today. They would, however, have been smaller – possibly a couple of inches shorter than us on average.

What age could they expect to live to?

They probably had a considerably shorter life expectancy than we do – because of disease, infant mortality and the lack of surgical knowledge. This would mean the most vigorous members of the community would have been in their twenties. It was probably quite rare to live much beyond forty.

Where did these people originally come from?

Our best guess is that these people came from the mainland of Scotland. They probably moved to Orkney because of the need for more land. Agricultural living allows population to grow; and this means people must travel to find new areas to farm.

Did they make war?

No weapons were found. And the village isn't sited for easy defence. So we don't think they were a warlike people. Their ways of resolving conflict were peaceful.

Could they write?

We are fairly sure they didn't have a system of writing – they wouldn't have needed one. Information would have been passed down from generation to generation by word of mouth.

Is there any evidence of human sacrifice?

None.

A WORLD HERITAGE SITE

Every community on earth is being deprived of an ancient necessary nourishment.
We cannot live fully without the treasury our ancestors have left us.
Without the story – in which everyone living, unborn, and dead, participates –
men are no more than 'bits of paper blown on the cold wind …'

(George Mackay Brown, *Portrait of Orkney, 1981*)

In December 1999 Skara Brae was inscribed upon the World Heritage List of the
Convention concerning the Protection of the World Cultural and Natural Heritage.
Inscription on this List confirms the exceptional universal quality of a cultural or natural site
which deserves protection for the benefit of humanity.
Together with other Historic Scotland properties – at Maes Howe, the Stones of Stenness
and the Ring of Brogar – Skara Brae forms part of The Heart of Neolithic Orkney World
Heritage Site. These monuments demonstrate the domestic, ritual and burial practices of a
5000-year-old culture with exceptional completeness.

View of Maes Howe (right foreground), the Stones of Stenness (left) and the Ring of Brogar
(right) with the lochs of Harray and Stenness and the landscape beyond (Farrer, 1862).